T0170988

Straight Talk with the Family

God's Blueprint for Strengthening the Family

Rev. Dr. Donald R. Wesson

Order this book online at www.trafford.com
or email orders@trafford.com

Most Trafford titles are also available at major online book retailers.

Printed in the United States of America.

ISBN: 978-1-4269-3670-8 (sc)
ISBN: 978-1-4269-3671-5 (e)

Our mission is to efficiently provide the world's finest, most comprehensive book publishing service, enabling every author to experience success. To find out how to publish your book, your way, and have it available worldwide, visit us online at www.trafford.com

Trafford rev. 10/07/2010

www.trafford.com

North America & international
toll-free: 1 888 232 4444 (USA & Canada)
phone: 250 383 6864 • fax: 812 355 4082

Table of Contents

Introduction

Family is the bond, the life force that holds the heart of man together. It is sad to say that the family that once was, is no more. There used to be a time when families came together each day. That time was dinner time, and all day on Sunday. Now we have twenty first century families living like gazelles, running to stay alive, never having time for the family, the one institution that God ordained from the beginning of time with Adam and Eve.

I believe that our microwave life style is the cause of our youth being lost to crime, sex, drugs, disrespectfulness, disobedience, and sinful living. Don't get me wrong, I am not putting the blame on our youth as much as I am on parents. Some parents have forgotten the role of a parent or failed to be educated on how or what it takes to be a parent. Anyone can have children, but not everyone can raise children. It takes a sculptor's love, heart and vision for his sculpture, to achieve his masterpiece, and it takes a parent's love, heart, and vision, to achieve their masterpiece.

The following passages of scripture bring us back to the responsibility of the parent to the family.

- *Teach your children to choose the right path, and when they are older, they will remain upon it. Proverbs 22:6 (NLT)*

- *These older women must train the younger women to love their husbands and their children, to live wisely and be pure, to take care of their homes, to do good, and be submissive to their own husbands. Then they will not bring shame on the word of God Titus 2:4-5, (NLT).*

- *In the same way, encourage the young men to live wisely in all they do. And you yourself must be an example to them by doing good deeds of every kind. Let everything you do reflect the integrity and seriousness of your teaching. Let your teaching be so correct that it can't be criticized. Then those who want to argue will be ashamed because they won't have anything bad to say about us, Titus 2:6-8, (NLT).*

The responsibility of the parent to the family is to train the family members in the way they should go, not the way they choose to go. This leaves no room for compromise. When we compromise as parents we weaken the very fabric of our family.

I can remember a time that my son spoke to me about his best friend coming to stay over one night. That night turned into four nights. I began to speak to my wife about this matter and her reply was, "It's okay." No, it was not okay for this young man who was just separated from his wife, and refused to stay at his mother's home, to stay with us. He had just become a compromising factor for my family. He spoke of an apartment opening up for him in a day. That never happened. I spoke up and said it was time for this young man to go and fix his marriage and stand up before his children and stop hiding out in my home. This helped me to understand that some parents have failed to teach their children how to build a strong family.

I remember watching a movie and there was a scene where a daughter left her husband and returned to her parent's home. She began to go out like she was a single woman. Her mother told her that she believed that it was time for her to go home to her husband, because whatever the problem, a husband and wife can work it out if they try.

Throughout this book you will find particular scriptures discussed more than once to address different aspects on the family.

Chapter 1

Developing a Transparent Family

Here the word *transparent* means don't hide behind your faults. Parents, if your families, are going to have any chance of healthiness, or any type of fullness, you and your children must not hide your faults.

If we hide behind our faults, how will family members ever learn about each other and how will we ever learn to minister to each others needs? We, as parents, have a tendency to hide our past and allow our children to duplicate our mistakes. This is not God's design for the family.

To produce a healthy family we must learn from our past and be better equipped for our future. A strong family must know what challenges it has overcome and what experiences and opportunities it has been afforded. We must learn to talk to each other rather than hide from each other.

I am reminded of an individual that came to me about ten years ago and shared with me that he hated his parents because of what he had learned about them as young adults. This individual was having a hard time because he had always believed that he had perfect parents, and that he was the one screwing up the family that his parents worked so hard to build.

His life was full of regrets and harshness for the lifestyle he was living, but he found out that his parents had some skeletons in their closets. If they had communicated openly about their skeletons, it could have helped him to understand that in life we all make mistakes.

He no longer felt he did not measure up as a man or a parent. He just wanted to be sure his children did not make the same mistakes he had. His question was, "Pastor Wesson, how do I fulfill this task, with my children?"

My response covered three areas of our lives which lead to transparency: one, we must get naked (be open and truthful); two, don't judge me; and three, I have been there so you don't have to go.

Each of these areas will help your children see the good and the bad in life, but the best part of this is that you remain in their lives to help shape and mold them into productive individuals. *Confess your sins to each other and pray for each so that you may be healed. The earnest prayer of a righteous person has great power and wonderful results* James 5:16, (NLT).

When we learn to share our faults and our skeletons with each other, we will find that it sets the person doing the sharing free from the guilt, the hurt, and the stress of it. The openness builds a greater bond between the family members. We should never allow anything to separate our family from the unity that we have worked so hard to achieve.

Parents, think of it this way, if you hide your mistakes from your children are you setting them up to become prey or victims?

I am not sure about what you desire for your family, but for mine, I never want my children or my wife left in a position to be overtaken by mistakes. Whatever happens to them has happened to me.

Transparency

Here are three helpful hints for becoming transparent, uncovering your stuff.

1. Let's get naked.

    This is about us as parents as well as the children in the family taking off the masks, removing the superman capes, pulling off the robes of deception, taking down the walls of tough guy, replacing the rose colored glasses of illusion, and finally laying to rest the facade that everything is well.

    Getting naked is really just exposing your weaknesses and downfalls before your family. This helps the members of the family understand that when I am at home with my family I can be real and I can get the proper support even when I don't receive it away from home.

    When your child comes in from school or a friend's home and you, as the parent, find out that he or she has been hiding things from you, you come down on him not for the mistakes he made, but because he did not trust you enough to talk with you about the issues.

And why should he talk with you when you taught him this type of behavior? He saw you, dad and mom, fighting and yet you acted as if nothing was wrong. He saw you, mom, making excuses for dad and his lack of concern about the condition of the family, and yet you both made it seem ok. These actions as well as others send mixed messages to your child about how he should conduct himself at home when he becomes a parent.

Parents, if we fail to demonstrate truth before our children it becomes an integrity problem. A lack of integrity is shown when parents refuse to allow their children to see real life and its struggles. The family bond is compromised by a lack of integrity.

Family is the living force to any man. When that force is hindered by lies, deception, cover-ups, and illusions, the family unit becomes dysfunctional. At this point the family unit operates differently than the way it was created to work.

Paul says to us in 2 Corinthians 10:4 (KJV), *For the weapons of our warfare are not carnal, but mighty through God to the pulling down of strongholds.* When we continue to allow past behavior (sin) to linger in our lives, it becomes a stronghold.

Strongholds are negative attributes such as pride, fear, insecurities, embarrassments, and denials. These forces work against God's will for man. If we allow these negative attributes, to continue to operate they become strongholds.

We break strongholds by releasing them to God and talking about them with our family. How do we release them to God, you may ask? John 8:36, (KJV). *If the Son, therefore shall make you free, ye shall be free indeed.*

So let's get naked; I did, about twelve years ago, with my family. It was more for my children than my wife. My spouse knew my shortcomings and why, but my children had no idea. I did not want my children duplicating my faults, nor did I want them to ever walk around with these types of weights or strongholds in their lives (lying, pride, insecurities, and not knowing who they are or where they came from). I live for them to be free in Christ Jesus, so I must lead the way to freedom, and I must show them how to attain it. We attain this through surrendering our lives and our wills to God. As parents we become transparent with our children.

2. Don't judge me.

Don't put me down for my faults. I am having a hard enough time dealing with them and openly sharing them.

The last thing I need is to have more condemnation piled on me. I desperately need forgiveness and grace extended to me.

Jesus said in Matthew 7:1-2, (NLT) *Stop judging others, and you will not be judged. For others will treat you as you treat them. Whatever measure you use in judging others, it will be used to measure how you are judged.* We all have to be careful how we look at another person's faults because some day we will have some faults of our own.

I think of some of the counseling sessions I have had, sitting with couples and sometimes their children. One may begin to confess his faults and explain why he refused to allow anyone to get close to him. Some would tell why they had been failing as fathers or mothers, and the children or the spouse would rip into them for their faults. That reaction only opened up a can of finger pointing and family division.

In many cases, the parents or the children have already condemned themselves. The love one needed family forgiveness, grace, mercy and given unconditionally.

3. I have been there, so you don't have to go!

How do we get this over to our children, and what are we actually speaking about when we make such a statement? If you really don't know or are confused about how to address an issue properly, think of the position that your family members are in.

Paul wanted the church to understand that he understood where they were spiritually, by observing what they were producing physically. *We all have sinned and come short of the glory of God,* Romans 3:23, (KJV).

Every sin has a name. When you decide to deal with your child using this term (sin), rest assured you are not alone. I have been there and done that. You must be specific about what you are saying. Discuss the **behavior,** the **mind set,** and the **attitude** of the individual. If you are going to be transparent, if you are going to get naked, and if you don't want your family members judging you, you must speak to their condition from your own personal experiences. You must reveal the behavior and attitude that you displayed, and how you became disobedient because you thought you knew what was best.

Every wife, every child, and every husband, want their conditions spoken to, and not just the symptoms. You cannot do this unless you understand and have knowledge of your past. When you have been there, you usually understand the condition your loved one is in. That is the time when you say, "I've been there so you don't have to go" and explain what you mean by this. Your loved one will receive it and benefit from it.

God often allows us to go through tough things so that we can be a helper to someone else. *But I have prayed for thee, that thy faith fail not: and when thou art converted, strengthen thy brethren,* Luke 22:32, (KJV).

Son, daughter, I have been insecure, had low self esteem, depending on others and wanting to be accepted. I had to look to God for my help. I could not escape the environment I was living in. The more I wanted out, it was like a force pulling me in. More and more I was losing my identity and my real personality in the things I was hiding in, to cover up my real problems.

I went through this, so you don't have to. You have some one to talk to. I promise that I will listen to you and then help you by sharing similar situations I have experienced. I am willing to do this because I don't want you to ever have to go through life feeling alone, or feeling that no one else cares what is going on with you. You have me as an example and I have you as a student.

Father God, you are the potter and we are the clay, shape, our family in your own miraculous way.

Chapter 2

Dad's Straight Talk to the Family

And they that shall be of thee shall build the old waste places: thou shall raise up the foundations of many generations, and thou shall be called, The repairers of the breach, The restorer of paths to dwell in, Isaiah 58:12, (KJV).

My Family Is Broken

Over the last 12 years I have painfully spent time conducting and officiating funeral ceremonies for multiple gang members. It was painful for two reasons. First, they were all young men under the age of 25. Second, it was painful because of the brokenness that the families had to endure.

These families were not broken because of their children's gang affiliations. They were broken because they lost the identity of their families and they do not understand the role each member was to play.

The family is like a team, every member has a position, and everyone must play their position if the team is going to win. Let's take a look at the team called the family. In this family you have the father. He is either in the home or out of the home. Then there is the mother; she too may be in the home or out of the home but she is more likely to be in the home. Then there are the children who have no choice but to be in the home. Each of these members develops a history with what we call family. Let's look at each position and see what it brings to the table.

Mom

The mother loves her children almost more than life itself. She births them into the world and she is grateful to God for her children. It does not matter if they are boys or girls, she is a proud mother.

No respectful mother brings her child into this world with the idea that her child will be a gang member, a thug, or an out of control youth. That mother sees a bright future for her child and begins to make plans for the success of the child's life.

As the child begins to grow, if it is a boy, the mother nurtures him, dresses him, loves him and hopes that he may grow into a productive young man. The only problem with this is that after this young man reaches the age of 10, some mothers begin to love their sons and the raising stops. I believe that mothers in our society today love their sons and raise their daughters. What do I mean by this? Sons are raised from birth to about the age of 10. Mothers, instruct their sons how to do things, teach them how to walk, how to speak, how to eat, how to dress themselves, how to bathe themselves and brush their teeth. They even teach them how to say yes, no, thank you and no thank you. With all of this the young male child is following the direction of the coach, his mother.

The breakdown comes when mom forgets that this boy will soon become a teenager with aggression, curiosities and peer pressure in his life. At that point the boy needs to know more about what to do and what not to do, along with what to watch out for. This is the area where a lot of mothers stop raising their sons and just start loving them.

Mothers don't usually hold their sons accountable to live within the confines of their teachings. The son begins to be curious about what life has to offer at that point and time in his life. He is faced with peer pressure, but he rarely comes home and talks to mom about it. Frequently, mom is not aware of to the challenges her son faces.

He is changing right before her eyes and she equates that to him just being a normal boy, not acknowledging that he is transitioning into a young man. If it was her daughter she would probably stop her and teach her the proper way to do things. She would tell her who she can and cannot hang out with, who she can and cannot date, how she should conduct her self on a date, and what to watch out for while she is on that date. This is not the case for her son. He may get into trouble, and in many instances mom will not confront him and may even reward him afterwards.

Soon this young man finds himself faced with a hard decision. Often it is this: "If I am going to hang out with my friends and be considered one of the boys I have to accept their lifestyle. I cannot go back and tell my mother about this. I am a man and not a chump." Mom finds out later that her son is involved in some unhealthy activities, and she tries to talk to him about her concerns and her pain. By this time he cannot afford to walk away even though he may never tell her that. Now mom is trying to figure out, "How did this happen?"

Mom, it happened because you stopped holding your child accountable for his actions. Likely you stopped using the disciplinary system you used when he was younger. Most of all you probably looked at your son as a young man. You thought he needed some space because some of his behaviors were telling you that a transformation was taking place in his life. You chalked it up to, "He is just growing up, he will be alright." That turned out, not to be the case. He became a wound to the family and your worst nightmare. This is never the way mom wants her son to turn out. No mother desires her son to grow up hustling, shooting, fighting, dealing or using dope and loving the boys more than loving his blood family.

Mom, it's not all on you, there is a greater problem that exists. The young man may feel he has to live in his father's shoes. Sadly, you probably never saw that reality coming, so you did not prepare yourself or your children for it. Mom is usually unequipped to deal with the fact that dad may not play his position properly or maybe neglecting his position completely. So Mom, if you invest the same amount of time raising him as you do loving him there is a good chance your son will not duplicate what his dad is or is not.

Dad

Dad, most likely you were proud to say, "This is my son or daddy's little girl". For the first few years, you walked around wearing the birth of your child as a badge of honor, and rightly so. But, when the child began to grow-up, you began to hit and miss on your hugs, on your time, on your words of wisdom, on your teachings and on saying "I love you."

The daughter is covered for a while because mom is there and she is raising her to become a wonderful young lady. But, the son keeps looking around the corner for you and you fail to appear. As a result he may be left with your legacy of street life, gang affiliation, and your rap as a hustler and womanizer. Most of all, your son may suffer from the lack of bonding with his dad.

Your son finds a replacement for you. It might be the big homie in the neighborhood who introduces your son to hustling, dealing and using drugs, having sex with multiple partners and gang banging. This creates a sense of false identity and a search for connecting or belonging to someone and something.

Dad, you forgot to raise your son. While you were out doing your thing, or as one might say, "doing you," your son was at home searching for you and found you in someone who only had false love for him.

After being absent from his son's life for years, dad sometimes desires to reclaim his position as father hoping to have an active role. By this time the son has probably filled the void in his life with his own lifestyle, whether good or bad.

The son may have traded dad in for a new lifestyle that was there for him when he was having hard times, when he needed someone to talk to, when he needed that sense of belonging. His lifestyle was always there for him. This lifestyle may very well be the death of him, but as one gentleman said to me, "We all have to die from something one day, so let him figure it out for himself. I did."

Dad, according to your model, your son may have learned it is ok to deceive people and make them think that you love them when in your heart you do not mean it. Watching you, your son may come to believe it is ok to run from the responsibilities of raising your children. Hanging with the boys, striving for a new tax bracket, or setting your goal to leave your mark on people's hearts is irresponsible. While you are giving your time, love, money, and attention to something or someone else, your family is left starving and fending for themselves. Starvation may occur physically, emotionally and socially, having devastating effects on your family.

Please don't misunderstand me. This chapter is written for the dads who have failed to maintain their roles and fulfill their responsibilities. Dad, your son or daughter will bond with something or someone other than you when they look up and don't see you there with outstretched arms.

Dad, your first responsibility is to work on your home. Your attention and love should always be focused on home. If you are going to hang out, why not hang out with people who love you and will allow you to be you? It does not matter what color you are or where you live, what type of job you have, corporate or McDonalds. The cries are all the same, "Daddy, will you be there to protect me from life's pains?"

Daughter

Daughters are always looked upon as being innocent and loving. A daughter is always known as daddy's little girl, and momma's heart. When she is small, she is everyone's little doll. As she begins to grow momma begins to instruct her how to sit, how to walk, how to speak, and in her teen years, how to date. Dad, in many cases, has very little to do with the grooming of his daughter, and when she needs to talk about dating from a male perspective, dad may shy away and leave the explaining to someone else.

Too often in our society today parents are out of touch with their children. Many young ladies find themselves looking for that bad boy type of individual who has a sculptured body, his pants below his waist and his underwear hanging over his pants.

She finds herself looking to her boyfriend for the love she desired from her father. My daughter, even at the age of 21, looked for me to hug her, to tell her that I loved her, and to be the man who could speak wholeness into her life.

You see, Dad, you should be the first man in her life who told her that you loved her. It should be you who held her with assurance. As a little girl, it was your touch that made her feel safe, and now that she is older, some stranger has taken your place. He may be a sports jock, a brain, or a young man who is rough around the edges. She still tries to find you in him. She is looking for reassurance, that manly voice that says, "I am here for you."

You must understand that mom sometimes has lost herself in being her daughter's friend. So, you have to stand up and be the man. If you fail to do this and mom moves into the role of friend, your daughter will find someone to play your roles. It may be an older young lady who will give her womanly advice or the young man who will serve as that new man in her life. Neither of them truly loves your daughter nor do they know what she is missing and longing for. They may have their own misguided agendas and your daughter's life is probably not a priority to them.

Your daughter may find herself chasing fads, submitting to peer pressure and having sex because she is in search of an intimate love relationship. So often the daughter will turn to substitutes, whether it is a man or a woman. It's all because she is looking for that reassurance, that touch of love and that sense of acceptance. She is dealing with hurts, voids, questions about her beauty and wondering if folks like her for her or for what she has to offer. If her parents are not there with outstretched arms, a tough life is truly ahead.

Son

Sons are the pride of their parents' hearts when they first enter this world. Parents don't really consider the future at that point. They don't think about whether their child will have to struggle or if their child will be a great man, or a misguided human being. They are just excited that God has blessed them with a healthy baby boy.

As their son begins to grow the father wants the world to know that his son is his little masterpiece, his newness of life. The son becomes his mother's little man, her champion, her opportunity to shape him into a man she would be proud of.

When the child grows into a toddler dad may slowly become estranged. Mom begins to love and train him how to speak, dress himself, read and write. As the son grows from the toddler stage to childhood stage, school age, dad grows even further away. He is tied up in his work, in weekend sports, hanging with the guys without his son. The son is now left at home with mom who tries to help him with his homework, fixes his meals, and sets his clothes out for tomorrow.

This is adequate for the moment but soon much more is required from the dad than from mom. The son now is moving into his teen years and needs to know what that funny feeling means when he is thinking about a girl. He is too embarrassed to ask his mother, and now he can't find his father. So he searches it out for himself from observing that manly connection that his dad has with his friends.

Then the time arrives when dad might be living in another home. Mom's hurt has turned to bitterness, and the son is left trying to put it all together. He asks, "Why is it, that mom has to be the one to take me to practice? Why is it that my father never comes around? What do I do now that I am faced with hard decisions about being a young man, and what is expected of me?"

In his search he realizes that it takes dad's wisdom. Dad is not around and all he has is his mother. He does not want to be labeled as a "momma's boy," so he decides he should figure this out on his own.

He talks to his boy in the neighborhood who quietly is in search of the same thing. Before long he finds himself like so many other inner city kids, searching for answers.

Many of them never find the answers even though they search high and low. They look into gangs, drugs, sex, and idolizing others, but even these do not give them the answers they are searching for.

One thing they do find, is death by the hands of another. When death comes it is then that those who are left behind get to hear resolutions as the preacher stands to speak words over their friend. I can hear the preacher as he stands and says to the audience, "I want to speak about the 'Inner City Kids.'"

O, awesome child of God
I pray these things for you
That you've learned who you are in Christ
Now that you know the truth
It doesn't matter where you come from
Or that you don't have worldly things
Because you were made with God's own breath
The sons and daughters of a king
God has a place reserved
In heaven, way up above
But while you're on this earth
He'll shower you with love
You belong to God's gang
The streets are not your home
You're covered by the blood
So the devil must leave you alone
Oh, but he'll come knocking!

And he'll try hard to make it in
But just kick him in the teeth
And tell him you hate sin!
And when he tries to buy you
With worldly goods and all his greed
Be sure you let him know
That Jesus meets your needs
If he still comes knocking
Don't believe his lies anymore
Just grab the hand of Jesus
And quickly slam the door
The devil, he can't stick around
If you resist him, he must flee
You're not a slave to sin
Because you have been set free!
So now you must go back
To the town in which you live
And spread the news to everyone
That you're God's Inner City Kids!

From *A Date with Grace*, pages 238 and 239
Donald Wesson, Author

It is sad that the only time that young men get a sense of love from their parents is when tragedy has fallen on their family or on one so close and dear. It is so amazing that at that very moment the boy finds what he is looking for, his family.

Everything we need to help us repair our broken families is in God's merciful hands. This is why we must continue in his master plan for the family.

Remember this thought from a poem entitled "Broken Things" in *A Date with Grace*, page 34.

It seems when something is broken
And I take it to be fixed
It's hard to leave it there
'Cause I want it back so quick
When there's something that I want
And I present my request to you
Then you tell me I'm not ready
To receive it, and it's true!
So off I go again
I try to get it on my own
Instead of being patient
Instead of leaving it alone
And then I've got a mess
Because I've done things my own way
And then I'm in a panic
But you tell me it's okay
You say, "Come back, we'll fix it
But this time, child, please wait
Have some faith in me
And things will turn out great."

Faced with Hopelessness

Epidemic is the word that comes to my mind when I think about the number of broken homes in our society. The father may be out of the home for reasons such as divorce, extra marital affairs, alcoholism, drug abuse, hobbies, clubs, or wrong associations. The mother may be struggling to do the best she can to raise her children. Mom works hard every day to keep food on the table and clothes on the backs of her children. Mom tries to meet every need for her family in the midst of deep hurt and pain, with feelings of emptiness.

Neglected children are the losers in the family because dad is missing in action, mom is stressing over her role and the parenting of the children is less than desirable. These children find themselves working things out among themselves. This type of life style is destined to be faced with hopelessness.

I believe that there are two conditions that result in hopelessness;

1. Living without any responsibility to God

2. Lack of intimacy among family members

You may ask, what does hopelessness look like? Roughly 14 years ago, I remember speaking with a young woman, I'll call Anna. She was doing a fine job with her five children as a single mom. She was a very hard worker, and worked long hours just to meet the needs of her children. She did not receive any assistance from their father who was MIA (missing in action) in every way.

As fate would have it the children were about to be abandoned and faced with loss again. Anna, was about to be faced with selfishness, loneliness, and dependency. She explained that she needed a man in her life for her sons. Their father was not around to help raise them and they needed that male influence in their lives right then.

I shared with her, that if this was not God's will for her and her children, she would be better off staying alone rather than having someone who was loved only to serve herpurpose. She replied that she believed God had given this man to her and she loved him as well. I asked her, would God give her a man who had failed to help raise his own son who was just a couple of years younger than her youngest son? She replied that it was not my problem, nor my worry. She was thinking of herself. I told her, it was a bit selfish and arrogant on her part. Anna was selling out her children for a man. If he would not support his own child, what could she expect him to do for her sons?

Long story short, she married the man and lost her children. The boys went to the streets and the daughter repeated Anna's lifestyle. The boys were then faced with the loss of their mother, her personal care, and her support. They were very athletic and good students. Because of the lack of parenting, guidance and responsibility along with the lack of accountability, the boys duplicated their father's lifestyle. The daughter duplicated her mother's lifestyle. She had a couple of children by one man and ended up with another man who did not work nor care for her children.

Here is another look at hopelessness, and this one will always stick with me.

The place is Bakersfield, California, where the city is divided into the haves and the have nots. In this city, there was a young man who was totally lost. Like so many other people in the world, he was without a father or a father figure who could give him direction for his life.

This young man had athletic and technical skills. In fact before he dropped out of high school during his freshman year, he had a 3.9 grade point average. This young man was floating through life, with low self esteem, an empty future and a sense of not belonging.

His father was not in his life. His mother was struggling hard with the care of his four siblings. The only thing that made him feel alive was what took place in the streets with his peers and those who were older. The streets, was the only place he could find a connection, or phileo love. His real lessons about life took place in the streets.

I sat down with this young man after a funeral I officiated. He was 15 years old at the time. I asked him about his future and the goals he set for himself. He began to explain that his future was trying to stay alive and out of prison. He said he didn't have a home,he had a house he lived in with his mom. She worked very hard to take care of his little brothers and sisters and it seemed as if there was never enough money.

He recalled one time his mom was going to lose their home because there wasn't enough money. He stated that he tracked down the man who was suppose to be his father and asked him for some money so they could keep their house. His father told him "I don't have it boy, if you want some money then you better get out and get yourself a hustle, for nothing is free."

At that point, at age 13 he made the decision to never allow anyone to take anything from him or his mother ever again. "Oh by the way Rev. it was my father who started me to selling drugs."

I will never forget a statement that he shared with me, "Pastor, there are a lot of young guys like me out here, who have made choices like me, because of their family life. We are not stupid at all, we have realized that we have to do what we have to do to survive."

I am glad to say that through my mentoring over the last year and a half, he has returned to school and is working on a real job. He is also on target to graduate his senior year. He has already passed his exit exams. He is now dreaming of becoming a Supreme Court Judge. There is hope for the Hopeless, if someone helps them dream again.

In the following chapters you will find helpful advice to keep your family from being victimized by brokenness and hopelessness.

Father please hear our cry, and heal our hurts and make provisions for our needs. Amen

Chapter 3

Sabbaticals Can Be Dangerous

I remember, back in the early 2000s my beloved daughter, Ashley, reminded me that when you fail to be mindful of your family, you can come home one day and find that your family has moved on in life without you.

Sabbatical is a term often used for a college professor who takes a leave of absence, usually after 7 years. He leaves his class room to do research in his field of interest. I would like to use this platform to help us recognize and return to the very principles or design God has set for the family.

Our families are surrounded by so many demands, so many requirements, so many distractions that the family members forget they have a responsibility to each other and that God holds us accountable to these responsibilities. This responsibility is to build up one another spiritually. *Husbands, love your wives, even as Christ also loved the church*

, and gave himself for it; Ephesians 5:25, (KJV). Wives, submit yourselves unto your own husbands, as unto the Lord Ephesians 5:22, (KJV); *Children obey your parents in the Lord, parents,* Ephesians 6:1, (KJV); *train up a child in the way he should go.* Proverb 22:6, (KJV)

How is this possible to meet our responsibilities when all of our service, time, and energy are poured out somewhere else other than at home?

Over the last twenty years of ministry I have come to understand that family members hypothetically go on sabbaticals everyday at school, work, in ministry, etc. Each of these areas call for individuals of your household to spend at least seven hours or more away from other family members and at the end of the day, the family has only fragments to share with one another.

When a child grows up without leadership from the parents his life will lack spiritual deposits, resulting in zero to minimum spiritual structure or growth. Ephesians 4:12 (KJV) says, *For the perfecting of the saints, for the work of the ministry, for the edifying of the body of Christ.* It is our job to build one another up. How can we build up, strengthen, or even edify one another if we return home from a day of achievement, a day of hustle and bustle, a day of stress, a day of anxiety or a day filled with exhaustion, with nothing left for one of the highest priorities God has given to us, our families?

I believe that when a professor leaves on his sabbatical he leaves with his job, school, and students as the main priorities for his study and his research. When he returns to his place of responsibility, he reaches out to meet the needs of his students.

What the professor has experienced is designed to equip him for such a time of accountability for his students, by meeting their needs for education, and equipping them for their goals and dreams for life. Yes, we too must understand that our family members have needs and they are looking to us to help fulfill their needs. This is achieved when we analyze our priorities. Too often our priorities are neither God focused nor family structured from a biblical standpoint.

Today, when we look at the design God left for families we find that families have forgotten what is really important for them.

The reason for a sabbatical should be to enhance the spirituality of the family members. A sabbatical should result in the family becoming God centered and goal oriented. Paying the mortgage, utility bills, food bills, clothing bills, or even education expenses are not adequate reasons to take a sabbatical.

Father God, help us to be more God focused, as we strive to be a blessing to our family.

Chapter 4

God Centeredness

In all thy ways acknowledge him, and he shall direct thy path.

Proverbs 3:5, 6 (KJV)

When we find ourselves walking in the path of God's instructions we will find that Paul's writings are true and that they work for us. In Philippians 1:8 (KJV) Paul said, *For God is my record, how greatly I long after you all in the bowels of Jesus Christ.* This is the very desire that we should have towards our family. I long to see you, my child, my mother, my father, my husband, or wife.

Our time away from one another should cause a longing to take place in our hearts. A longing that causes us to seek God's face during the course of the day as well as during the time to and from work, school, or wherever we have spent our time out of the presence of our families. We should ask, "What is it that my family needs of me today? How can I worship you, God, through service to my family?"

God is the creator of the family and He has designed specific responsibilities for each family member. God instructs husbands; *Husbands, love your wives, even as Christ also loved the church, and gave himself for it* (Ephesians 5:25, KJV); God instructs fathers; *And, ye fathers, provoke not your children to wrath: but bring them up in the nurture and admonition of the Lord* (Ephesians 6:4, KJV); God instructs wives; *Wives, submit yourselves unto your own husbands, as unto the Lord* (Ephesians 5:22 KJV); God instructs women; *to love their husbands, to love their children, To be discreet, chaste, keepers at home, good, obedient to their own husbands, that the word of God be not blasphemed* (Titus 2:4-5, KJV); And God instructs the children; *Children, obey your parents in the Lord: for this is right. Honour thy father and mother, which is the first commandment with promise; That it may be well with thee, and thou mayest live long on the earth* (Ephesians 6:1-3, KJV).

Every one has a job to do in the family but each member must keep themselves focused on God and God alone. I believe that this is what Jesus was conveying to us in John 15:1-3, (KJV); when he said, " *I am the true vine; and my Father is the husbandman. Every branch in me that beareth not fruit he taken away: and every branch that beareth fruit, he purgeth it; that it may bring forth more fruit. Now ye are clean through the word which I have spoken unto you.*

"Abide in me, and I in you. As the branch cannot bear fruit of itself, except it abide in the vine; no more can ye, except ye abide in me. I am the vine, ye are the branches: He that abideth in me, and I in him, the same bringeth forth much fruit: for without me ye can do nothing. If a man abide not in me, he is cast forth as

a branch, and is withered; and men gather them, and cast them into the fire, and they are burned. John 15:4-6, (KJV).

When, we must leave our places of research, experiences, and data gathering for the day, we must find ourselves focused on the Lord Jesus Christ and what he would have us share with our family members when we return home so that we will be a blessing to them. For this to happen we must be able to do the following things:

1. Receive what God has for us while we are on our Sabbatical.

2. Understand what we have received and how it is to be used to minister to our families.

3. Spend time in prayer before arriving home. Inquire what it is that God wants us to do when we arrive home.

4. Have a mind set that we will seek the blessings for our families rather than for ourselves.

We must remember the purpose of the sabbatical for the professor. He is conducting research for his students. We must work the work that God has given us for our families.

He came to the earth with us on His mind. Jesus went to the cross with us on His mind. He laid in the grave three long days with us on His mind. He took on the form of a man, after the fashion of a man, that he would experience what we would go through. This is why He can say to us in John 16:33 (KJV), *"but be of good cheer for I have overcome the world.* "This is a reassurance to us that anything that we might go through, or anything that might confront us, we can overcome. And Paul teaches us in Romans 8:28 (KJV). *And we know that all things work together for good to them who love God, to them who are the called according to His purpose.*

It is never about us, but always about our families.

Father God, bind our hearts together as we strive to fulfill your design for our families.

Chapter 5

Priorities

If we are going to be effective in reaching our family members, as well as utilizing our experiences with God, during our times away from our families there are some steps we must take. These steps are called Priorities. We must put our priorities in order, not the order that seems to be right, but the order according to God's structured principles.

- God's will, must always be first.
- Marriage, if you are married. If you are not married family is second.
- Family

This is the structure that God has given to his children.

Priority 1: God's will

Matthew 6:33, (KJV); But *seek ye first the kingdom of God, and his righteousness; and all these things shall be added unto you.*

David helps us in Proverbs 3:5- 6, (KJV); *Trust in the Lord with all thine heart, and lean not unto thy own understanding. In all thy ways acknowledge Him, and He shall direct thy paths.* Without God and His guidance through the Holy Spirit we will never be what our families need us to be.

Priority 2: Marriage

The husband and the wife are to be a blessing to each other before they can be a blessing to others. Paul teaches us in Ephesians 5:21 (KJV), *Submitting yourselves to one another in the fear of God.*

If God is not in the forefront of the marriage then it becomes impossible to build each other up. Mutual respect has to be one of the first tools used in the marriage. Secondly, love has to be ushered into the marriage. Ephesians 5:25 (KJV), *Husbands, love your wives even as Christ also loved the church, and* ***gave himself*** *for it.* Without the love of Jesus in our marriage we will find ourselves searching for something that only God can give and has given to the church. We may try to replace this love with money, cars, land, houses, and fame only to come up empty in the real love department.

Obedience is required, not according to what man has put into practice in this world, but according to what God has placed in his word. This obedience is speaking to the position and authority God has placed upon the husband. If the husband is practicing obedience in his walk with God and his role of leadership in the marriage, his wife will have no problem following his lead. Paul further teaches us in Ephesians 5:22, (KJV); *Wives, submit yourselves unto your own husbands, as onto the Lord.*

When our wives are walking in submission it is not to their husbands, but to the principles of God. Wives are not instructed to submit because we are great providers, hard workers, or loving fathers. As husbands, we set the standard and example that God's principles are to be obeyed in our marriages and homes.

Priority 3: Family

Our children, in most cases, will only live according to what they are taught by their parents. Children have no knowledge of God's ordered principles regarding their responsibility in the family. I believe this is why Paul left this writing for us in Ephesians 6:1 (KJV), *Children, obey your parents in the Lord, for this is right. Honour your father and mother, which is the first commandment with promise.*

Solomon brings a strong command to parents in Proverbs 22:6 (KJV), *Train up a child in the way he should go: and when he is old, he will not depart from it.* I believe this command makes it possible for us as parents to hold our children accountableto Ephesians 6:1-2 (KJV),

If the example of God's principles, have been properly modeled before the child, usually the child will live accordingly.

The Father's Responsibility in the Family

Paul instructs fathers to teach, to raise and instruct our children how to honor God through living according to his principles. Ephesians 6:4 (KJV), *And ye, fathers, provoke not your children to wrath; but bring them up in the nurture and admonition of the Lord.*

We train our children by example, living according to the word of God, and being obedient to God's word. Being an example of the word of God means to model the word of God. We model the word when we find ourselves searching for ways to serve others.

Here are some ways of achieving service to others:

- Use your vacation time to minister to one another.
- Schedule family conferences once a year.
- Wives should participate in a women's conference once a year.
- Husbands should participate in a men's conference once a year.
- Young people should participate in a youth summit conference once a year.

When I do this, it helps equip me to minister to my family. The professor attends many seminars, conferences, and workshops each year in addition to his sabbatical every seven years. So be it with the professor, so be it with us.

We are commanded to teach God's commandments as in Deuteronomy 6:7 (KJV); *And thou shalt teach them diligently unto thy children and shalt talk of them when thou sittest in thine house, and when thou walkest by the way, and when thou liest down, and when thou risest up.*

The Mother's Responsibility in the Family

She has the responsibility to assist the father to implement his instructions for the family. The mother is the nurturer of the family, she teach them how to love, how to show compassion, and displays a forgiving heart. She must train her children in followship, as the father leads the family should follow. A godly mother and wife striving for perfection may desire to model the example of the Proverbs 31 woman. Proverbs 31, describes everything good and perfect about womanhood; strong positive equalities, wisdom, love, compassion, many skills, industrious and resourceful. Her children stand blessing her. Her husband praises her. Proverbs 31:28, (NLT).

Sabbaticals for the Family, Helpful Hints, Applying Proverbs 3:5,6:

- Pray that God will unveil to you where he wants you to vacation, when and how to use this time to effectively minister to your family.
- Reestablish your family time, starting with one day a week and working toward seven days a week. You can even use an outside family activity, such as a sporting event, going to see a movie at a theater, etc.
- When departing from your family each day, for work, school, etc, seek God during the day for how he wants you to use your experiences to enhance your ability to minister to your family.
- As you return home ask God to help you shift from student, employee, employer, etc.. Ask God to show you how you can minister to the needs of your family members.

- Husbands and wives: don't forget to take time out during the evening to minister to each other by communicating about one another's needs.
- Pray for your family without ceasing.

Father God, help us as family members to set all things in order.

Chapter 6

Family Worship

Till we all come in the unity of the faith, and of the knowledge of the son of God, unto a perfect man, unto the measure of the stature of the fulness of Christ:

Ephesians 4:13 (KJV)

What is worship? you may ask. It is not what we have made it out to be in our society today.

Worship is more than just standing in the sanctuary [church building] waving our hands or shouting. It's more than just clapping our hands. Real worship is ushered out and comes from a state of intimacy. According to John 15:4 (NLT), *Remain in me, and I will remain in you. For a branch cannot produce fruit if it is severed from the vine, and you cannot be fruitful apart from me.*

Intimacy is an inward attribute that displays an outward expression. There has to be a heart to heart connection between us and God. Matthew 22:37 (KJV) states, *Jesus said unto him, Thou shalt love the Lord thy God with all thy heart, and with all thy soul, and with all thy mind.* Jesus requires love from all of us inwardly. When our love is offered up to Jesus and it becomes a lifestyle, God receives it as worship to him.

This is not the only way to worship God. Worship also requires our service, honor, and devotion. Worship from God's viewpoint is only accepted when we, his children, step into that which he has required of us in his word and do so according to his will.

He has designed the blueprint. It's our job to follow it. Family has been a part of God's plan from the beginning and nothing in this world can change that.

Service

John 15 tells us that we must abide in Christ. So, if we abide, then we stand in position to display his love to our love ones. When we do this it will cause our families to do the same.

I think back about ten years ago when I began to exercise this principle in my own home. I began to see the coming together of my family. We began to spend time every morning praying for each other's day, praying for God's provision for the day as we experience his will for each of us. I will never forget that my daughter, Ashley, had just begun Junior High School and she was having a tough time with her math class. She stated one morning that she believed that God was going to give her the victory over this class, so could we just believe God for the victory instead of asking Him for help? She explained that she had seen me and her mother walk in His victory through all we go through, regardless of the situation.

This only inspired me to worship the Lord even more through serving my family in every way I could. I found myself looking more and more into my family's heart, so much that I began to know them intimately. It became the same for them towards me.

What a blessing and awesome feeling when your children look bigger and are more important than an academic or athletic achievement. It is God who allows us the opportunity to experience what most families may only desire to experience.

This does not make my family any better than any other family. It's just that we allowed ourselves to grow past the outer shells of life and begin to see the spiritual blueprint God has for the family. God helped us to get past who, the Jones were and what they had, to see how we could focus on our family members individually and collectively. Our lives have not been the same since. In fact we continue to look for every opportunity to encourage and lift up each other.

I think back to a Thursday afternoon in 2002. My son, Givon, and I were driving to Bakersfield from Delano. We were just seven miles into our trip when I asked him, "Son, what's bothering you?" His reply was, "Nothing is going on. Why do you ask?" I answered, "Because I am feeling your spirit and something is troubling you." He then started crying and said, "I don't have a grandmother any more, and the only one I tried to reach out to as my grandmother was your mother and she is acting like she doesn't want to accept me as her grandson, and I don't know why. I have never done anything to her but tried to love her. She is the only grandparent I have left, and I don't know what to do."

I pulled off the freeway, sat to talk with him and prayed for him. My instruction to him was, "Son, you are never held accountable for what she does, or doesn't do, but God holds you accountable for what Givon does. Love your grandmother even as God continues to love us. Through his love you will find that God will do two things. One, he will always give you peace in the midst of your pain. Two, he will work on the heart of your grandmother, even as he worked on Jacob's heart before meeting with his bother, Esau. Esau's and Jacob's past life was full of turmoil, anger, lies and division. However, the importance of their reunion overshadowed the differences of their past. Son, don't let this challenge sidetrack you, but let it usher you right into a new level of growth, a growth that will help you experience a side of God that some people never experience. Son, I feel your pain and I want you to know I am here for you as you take on this journey. If you need me, I am here but most of all remember that Jesus is always present with you."

These are just a couple of testimonies that will help you understand what the basis of worship is about. Service to family members is an important part of family worship.

Honor

Honor, what is that? It's giving God the respect and recognition he deserves. How is that done? It is accomplished by honoring those in your household first. In Philippians 2:3 (KJV), Paul teaches us that we are to esteem others more highly than ourselves. Our children are the gifts that God has given to us to develop in his character and his likeness.

We must give respect and recognition to one another as family members regardless of age or gender. We must put each other first and hold each other up high in the sight and love of God.

I honor my wife. She wears many hats for our family; referee, instructor, provider, mother, advisor, homemaker, finance manager, chef, cheerleader, friend, lover, partner, and business woman. She deserves to be honored not just for the hats she wears. She must be honored because she is a lover of God and daily displays his attributes before her family which is her way of honoring God by giving true honor to her family spiritually.

I remember having a discussion with my queen (who is my wife). She spoke of the Proverbs 31 Woman. She felt no woman could fulfill all of Proverbs 31. She believed that a woman could do some of what she accomplished. I explained, to my queen, "My queen, that is not true. I have a Proverbs 31 Woman. God blessed me with you and you are my Proverb 31 Woman." My wife fulfilled every one of the areas the Proverbs 31 woman performed. Yes, I honor my queen as God's child and his gift to me.

I am a father of a blended family, but to know my family you would never know that we are a blended family. I honor all my children the same and with the same Godly love that is so freely given to me by God and my family.

I think about one of my sons, Jarvis. One day he and I had to face one of the most difficult times of our lives just as so many other parents and children have.

My son became a father before he became a husband. I will never forget that moment with him. It was a nice semi-warm day during the month of March. He arrived home and I called him to the dining room table and began to question him about him becoming a father. "Son," I said, "Can you tell me why you chose to do this and when were you going to talk to me about it?" His response was, "Daddy, I was afraid to tell you because of what you would have felt about it and me." I replied, "Have I set such a presence in your life that you feel that you cannot talk to me about anything? I am forever sorry for making you feel this way. Son, please understand me. I love you and thank God for you. Don't ever feel that you have to keep anything from me. I am here just for you, and whatever you are going through. It is my job to become your servant, in helping you to overcome, that God may get the glory and that you may grow from it."

At this time it became my responsibility to facilitate my son's development into a godly and a loving father. Even though, I was not happy to be a grandfather under those circumstances. However, I realized anger was not the solution. Parents please understand that "I told you so," and anger does not respect nor honor your child. Oh, I know my son did not show any honor or respect towards me as a parent. I experienced the same hurt and insecurity, my child was faced with. Understand that he had dishonored me as well as God. Also, understand this was not the time to say, "I told you so."

This is why worship is more than just standing in the church building waving my hands and shouting. True worship is about honoring God by allowing Him to demonstrate His love through me by showing His love and compassion for my child who is really His child.

Furthermore, how would my son learn to honor his child unless I became who Peter instructed me to become? Peter teaches us in 1 Peter 2:21 (KJV), *For even hereunto were ye called: because Christ also suffered for us, leaving us an example, that ye should follow his steps.* This is true honor in every sense of the word.

Worship, Helpful Hints:

- Don't be afraid to spend time in prayer with your family.
- Don't allow a bad situation to cause you to fall apart, but use it to teach compassion and godly love to your family.
- Take time to talk to your family and allow them to speak to you.
- Help your family understand that the father's role in the family is to be a servant to them (This does not mean to be a slave).
- Ask yourself if you had bad news to tell your parents how you would want them to take it. Then use that to minister to your family.
- Always take time to honor your family through the respect and recognition you give them.

Father God, teach us how to be more intimate with one another. Please teach us how to show each other your love and compassion.

Chapter 7

Family

What is family you ask? Family in our society today may be described in these ways:

1. From the marriage standpoint it is a man and a woman with a child or children.

2. It could be in some people's mind set that family is where a parent is in the home with a child or children, biological or step children (blended family).

3. For some family is in the work place.

4. Some often make our friends our family.

5. Some make their neighborhood gang friends their family.

> A family almost always requires someone who stands in the position of a parent, if not the biological parent, a step-parent, a foster parent, an aunt or uncle. Some times, even a facility like juvenile hall, youth authority or a group home may assume the role of a parent. Whoever or whatever functions as a parent usually has specific principles and rules they practice to develop their family.
>
> The question what is family has yet to be answered. I believe the frantic search for family, the desperate need to belong is why we have so many youth joining gangs, brotherhoods, and secret organizations looking for a male or female to love, having babies before marriage and career, and experiencing same sex relationships. They are in search of this great phenomenon, the family.

I do believe that there is an answer to this great phenomenon called the family. Let's explore a few areas in search of this answer.

This phenomenon, the family was designed by God, our creator. It was He who said to Adam and Eve, to be fruitful and multiply. Everything that was needed for love, hope, intimacy, support, belonging, respect and interdependence, was given to man by God. I have often heard comics make fun of the Huxtables, Father Knows Best, and other sitcoms like these. Their statement was that there are no, such families. I believe that we are looking at the wrong part of the movies. These sitcoms show accountability, responsibility, intimacy, transparency, respect, as well as esteeming other family members, and let's not leave out the challenge to have a college education, for it helps you to raise your sights about life.

As we look back at these shows and others like them, we find that the characteristics listed above are missing in our homes today. Why do I call the family a great phenomenon? Many are in search of something that God has given us the ability to experience, but we continue to look at man, teach what our parents and grandparents taught, but are never willing to teach what God has taught us about the family and how he designed it to operate for our good and his pleasure.

Structure

In every family, household or home there has to be structure (order). Paul helps us with this in 1 Corinthians 11:2-3 (KJV), *Now I praise you brethren, that ye remember me in all things, and keep the ordinances, as I delivered them to you.* (The word *ordinance* means an authoritative command or order). *But I would have you know, that the head of every man is Christ, and the head of every woman is the man, and the head of Christ is God.*

By no means does this imply that the woman is beneath the man. It is stating that man is the covering, the protector, the provider, and the sacrificial lamb for his wife and his family. And the wife/mother is the receiver, the balancer, and helper to her husband/father for the family.

The structure principles should be practiced continually. Women were put here for man's pleasure is an old cliché. This lie has caused men to see women in a different and degrading light. This thought process has taken us away from the original blueprint for men and women and their roles in the marriage and the family.

Any time we turn or change the blueprint, we are out of order and doomed to fail. Let's compare building a family to building a physical structure. If a contractor should decide to change the order of how a building is to be built, there could be some serious consequences. If the contractor decides to place the windows in before he puts the roof on there can be major problems. If he decides to plaster and color coat the outer walls before he hangs the sheet rock, he will face much cracking in the outer plastered walls. This is the case with the order found in 1 Corinthians 11, we must live according to the structure that has been set if we are going to positively experience the family as God designed it.

Respect

In Ephesians 5:21 (KJV), we read: *Submitting yourselves one to another in the fear of God.* In spite of our faults and failures and different backgrounds we are still to consider others more highly than ourselves.

There is no room for altering the structure. We must make every effort to follow it to the letter. Our society is suffering because we make up our own rules as we see fit or as they have been passed down from one generation to the next. By the time that we enter the area of the marriage or family we may be lost or confused and searching for something better but not finding it.

Respect goes for the whole household. *And ye, fathers, provoke not your children to wrath: but bring them up in the nurture and admonition of the Lord.* Ephesians 6:4 (KJV); We should clearly model respect to our children to the point that they will respect us and God. It all starts with us, mom and dad, husband and wife, and then children.

Respect is an attribute that is so often taken for granted and misunderstood. Respect is not a sign of weakness, but a sign of growth in humility.

It is often said that respect is earned and not just given. I believe that this is why our society is suffering with fragmented and dysfunctional families today. We have lost sight of respecting a person because he or she is a human being.

Respect starts with our families first, as Jesus instructs us in Acts 1:8 (KJV), *But ye shall receive power, after that the Holy Ghost is come upon you: and ye shall be witnesses unto me both in Jerusalem, and in all Judea, and in Samaria, and unto the uttermost part of the earth.* Jesus instructs us so we will be witnesses of who He is and the blueprint that God has laid out for us. We are living examples of respect when we demonstrate Jesus' lifestyle, His love, character, and intimacy, to our family members.

In my 17 years of pastoral ministry I have noted that parents have a tendency not to respect their children. The way parents, speak to their children, treat them, and respond to their behavior, clearly shows this. I can remember my father and mother had a saying that so many people use today, "Children are to be seen and not heard." What is the problem with this? Why would parents have a conversation around their children and not want them to chime in? Why would parents use, language they don't want their children to repeat? Why would a parent speak about their spouse or another person of the opposite sex in front of a child, and then tell them what is right and or wrong?

We are disrespecting our children when we raise them up under the instruction of *do as I say and not as I do.* Moreover, why would parents have their children in the home and not allow them to speak? How will you ever know what they are thinking? How would you ever teach them what respect is without interacting with them?

Peter teaches that we are to model respect for others in the household not because they give it to us or because we have earned it, rather, because that's what is required by God, *Feed the flock of God which is among you, taking the oversight thereof, not by constraint, but willingly; not for filthy lucre, but of a ready mind. Neither as being lords over God's heritage, but being ensamples to the flock.* 1 Peter 5:2-3, (KJV); Jesus states it this way, *For I have given you an example that ye should do as I have done to you.* John 13:15, (KJV).

Respect should be lived so others may learn what it is. Our children repeat what they have been taught. Their language, their disrespect and disobedience to their parents and those of authority are all learned behaviors.

Every football season, a brother of the church and I attend the high school football games. We experience the presence and the lack of home structure and respect. Some kids will stand up in front of you while you are trying to watch the game. It's not as if they are moving somewhere, they just stand to talk. When we ask them to sit down or move over so we can see the game they act as if we are not speaking to them or they will begin to use foul language. At times young ladies are sitting and talking and during their conversation they begin to use more profanity than I used when I was unsaved. This disrespectful behavior is most likely allowed at home. I have a thought and it goes like this, "Whatever one is allowed to do at home, they will do it away from home."

Our children must learn that when they are at home or when they leave home they represent their parents, and if they have a relationship with God, they also represent Him. Also parents must understand that when they are away from home that they represent their children and God if they have a relationship with Him. Nothing can embarrass and hurt children more than when their parents show a lack of respect in the way they speak and behave in public. The family always suffers from what family members do at home or away from home.

Father God, thank you, for my family. Now we are asking if you would help us to live as a godly family.

Chapter 8

The Family Is a Ministry

From whom the whole body fitly joined together and compacted by that which every joint supplieth, according to the effectual working in the measure of every part, maketh increase of the body unto the edifying of itself in love. Ephesians 4:16, (KJV).

For our comely parts have no need: but God hath tempered the body together, having given more abundant honour to that part which lacked: That there should be no schism in the body; but that the members should have the same care one for another. 1 Corinthians 12:24-25, (KJV).

Both readings in Ephesians and 1 Corinthians allude to the fact that each member has a responsibility to the family, from the oldest to the youngest. Age does not matter. God put each member in the family. Biological or blended, it is still a family that God has allowed to come together with a purpose.

This purpose is two fold. First, it is to honor and worship God as we walk according to the blueprint He has set for the family. God's blueprint will develop family members into servants, one to another. Secondly, it is for man to minister to the needs of each other as they operate in their gifts from God.

There are healthy and unhealthy ways to minister to the needs of the family. We will get to the differences in a moment. Please note that there is a way to live in the world and believe that you are ministering the right stuff to your family, when all along you are misguiding your family. Many believe their families are living according to God's blueprint and really ministering to the needs of their families because they attend church, work in the church, hold a position in the church or have attended the church for many years along with their parents and grandparents. This is far from the truth.

An Unhealthy Family

In the clinical world of counseling, unhealthiness in families is called *dysfunctional.* A family is described as dysfunctional when it operates in a manner contrary to its design.

We are faced with an epidemic in our society. Many children are allowed to be their own instructors of life. Before they even attain the knowledge of what life is or what their role is in the family they choose and pick what they will do with their lives. Affording children this right is encouraging them to live their lives recklessly.

Our children are into name brand clothing, expensive cars, clubbing, and having fun. They don't understand that there is a greater responsibility to their families. Our children grow up with idols and role models, but these usually are not their parents or siblings. Often their role models are professional athletes, movie stars and entertainers. Our children dress like them, our children measure success by them and our children live their lives to become them. It's becoming rare to hear children say, "I want to be like my father or mother". Parents should be the first real role models in their children's lives.

It is unhealthy for the family, when the children are star-struck. Many parents encourage and promote this type of behavior without explaining responsibilities and requirements of this type of lifestyle.

There was a time when parents taught polite and courteous behavior to their children, "Yes, Ma'am" and "Yes, Sir", "No, Ma'am" and "No, Sir" "Thanks" and "You are welcome." Today our children say "Yea," and "No," "Whatever," "My bad, or that's the bomb." In fact, we have commercials that show parents and grandparents trying to be hip, so they can say they are relating with their children.

The questions I have are: How does a parent being hip minister to the needs of children? How does that help the family walk in the blueprint that God has set for the family?

I want to share five points with you, the reader. Take these into consideration for identifying unhealthy practices in your family.

- Compromising

We compromise when we give our children their space without responsibilities and without accountability, for their actions. Children need their space to make their own decisions for their lives. However, children need to understand that the decisions they make may affect the whole family. Our world holds us responsible and accountable for what we do. If we break the law, there are consequences. If we fail to follow instructions, there are consequences.

Children should receive sound instructions and guidelines for their lives from their parents. This means that parents are to be all up in their business, holding them accountable for their actions and teaching them what responsibility means.

How can we measure our effectiveness as parents unless we know the mind of our children? How can the family function as one body unless everyone is walking by the same rule or blueprint? Parents, never trade in your principles for popularity or your parenting for friendship.

- Parenting

Solomon was the wisest man ever, so I believe that we should embrace his wisdom. *Train up a child in the way he should go: and when he is old, he will not depart from it.* Proverbs 22:6, (KJV); in this verse is one of the principles of God's blueprint for the family.

We as parents are sometimes too busy allowing our children to raise themselves after they reach the age of nine or ten years old. They choose their own clothes, shoes, and hair styles. Many times our children decide what they will have for dinner, or where they will have dinner. We allow our children to stay over night at a friend's home without really knowing what principles are being taught there.

One day my sons said to their mother, that they wished she was like a friend of theirs, whose mother was like a friend to him. Their mother elaborated on the fact that she was their mother, not their friend. Her God given responsibility was to be their mother, to teach them and raise them up according to God's word.

I then chimed in and explained, "If my wife treated our sons like her friends, how would they ever learn what a godly mother was and how would they ever learn how to minister to the needs of their children?"

Parents have very important roles in the family, and ifparents fail to fulfill their roles as designed by God, the family will suffer from the lack of training. Parents, we, are the leaders of the family and if the leaders fail to lead then how will the family members learn their roles?

Many parents today live with a guilt complex, "I want my child to have all the things that I had or did not have. I don't want my child suffering like we did." Or, "I can't allow my child to do without." "What would my parents and grandparents say?" So we start out with clothing, where we live, and then there is always the car, all of these coming without the main two principles and rules: responsibility and accountability.

We must set guidelines on our clothes, expectations on where we live and proper rules for the cars. If any of the rules are broken we must enforce accountability before our children. If we don't, we are setting up our children for behaviors, and lifestyles of disrespect and lack of integrity.

- Lack of Intimacy

We live in a day and time when families are not connected at the heart any longer. I heard a young lady voice the fact that she thought it was her mother's responsibility to send her to college. It was not what she said but how she said it. She had no idea what her parent had gone through for her and what it would take for her mother to send her to college.

Many children today, never consider others at all, it's all about them, never mind the parent or the family if they themselves are in need of something. As a family, we should think of the role of each member and how we can make life easier for that individual.

These days we call it the "miracle family" if that family has members who give of themselves for the benefit of others and do not think about how they will have to do without. There are children and parents in the family who turn to outsiders for some type of satisfaction. Some family members feel a great need to give to their family members. Giving with love and compassion are unique characteristics of the caring individual in the family. We have lost that type intimacy in the family. Things, sports, friends, cars, and popularity have become the attributes that we have substituted for intimacy.

When it comes to popular entertainers and professional athletes, children can usually tell you some very specific information like where they were born, how they were discovered, who they are married to, the colors they like, the struggles they have gone through and why they say the things they say. When it comes to the family many children have no idea why their parents refuse to allow them to participate in certain activities. Most children don't know half as much about their parents as they know about well known individuals as stated above.

Many kids feel they have to participate in the fads of tattoos, piercings and coloring their hair. They call it "finding themselves, or being their own person." It is now said that tattooing has become body art, it is expressing one's inner person.

We have melted God's blueprint down to body piercing and tattoos in order for a man to understand who he is. How can this be when the persons doing all of this foolishness have no idea who they really are? More and more the parents lose their intimate connection with their tattooed and pierced children. These children become strangers to their own families.

Paul says, *And be not conformed to this world: but be ye transformed by the renewing of your mind, that ye may prove what is that good, and acceptable, and prefect will of God.* Romans 12:2, (KJV). *Wherefore come out from among them, and be ye separated, saith the Lord, and touch not the unclean thing; and I will receive you.* 2 Corinthians 6:17, (KJV). A structured positive family life is almost always necessary to equip our children with tools and qualities that will enable them to differentiate between right and wrong. When the proper tools such as, prayer, studying the word, worship and praise and qualities like love, integrity, honesty, discipline, faith, commitment, responsibility and accountability are developed in our children they will be empowered to stand against the strong forces of peer pressure.

- Dating and Sex

This is the threshold to main stream society. It seems as if everybody is having sex. In fact, Hollywood has taken sex and dating to a whole new level. "Date someone who complements you." Too Many women, find their complement in that bad boy, or the thug, not the well educated brother or the hard working man, especially if he has a mediocre job.

Dating should be about learning about each other, or looking for that one special somebody who will be a good partner and a good parent with you someday. Dating, from a Christian point of view, is getting to know someone with Christian beliefs. I have never understood why Christians date unsaved men or women.

There are requirements for dating today. You must be prepared to have sex and bites all over your neck. The woman has to be prepared to be a sharing and caring kind of young lady. Most of our young men now believe in having sex with more than just one person. I know what you are thinking, "That's the way it is, he is not married just yet, and it happens."

I can think back several years ago when a young man and young lady started dating it was usually all about learning about one another and getting to know each other's family members. Six months to one year later, the couple would often make plans for marriage. After the two had spent time sharing, caring and connecting they made the decision that they were ready and willing to take each other as husband and wife.

Many couples date, shack up, and have sex to make every effort to connect with each other. The person that you are dating doesn't have to be accepted by your parents, nor do you need to be accepted by his or her parents. However, whenever it's possible to get acquainted with future in-laws you should take the opportunity.

It used to be that couples would encourage one another to get their educations, start their careers, and purchase their own places. Then with the approval of each set of parents the couple would then seek to be married.

People are so shallow that they go through all types of plastic surgeries to make themselves look beautiful. This goes for women as well as men. We have lost sight of the heart of a person, to focus on what one has physically, body parts, shape, size and what he or she has to offer. We seldom find ourselves looking and building from our hearts to the hearts of the men or women we love. Dating is the ideal time for couples to make that heart to heart connection that will result in intimacy.

Much disrespect exists and is tolerated in today's dating process. Blowing the horn for the date to come outside, dropping the date off without walking her to the door, cheating on one another, date rape, physical abuse, verbal abuse, emotional abuse, sex outside of marriage and children outside of marriage are just a few acts of disrespect that permeate the dating process.

It is God's design for parents to be examples setting standards and setting guidelines for our children. Proper, consistent structure and instruction will minimize the number of at risk children and maximize the number of children who will succeed.

- Relationship with God

Many people have a relationship with God but only a few walk in intimacy with God. The Bible lays it out this way, *They will act as if they are religious, but they will reject the power that could make them godly.* 2 Timothy 3:5, (NLT); In 2 Timothy 3:7 (KJV) we read, *Ever learning, and never able to come to the knowledge of the truth.*

Our families may go to church but that does not mean that there is a total surrendering to God's will, His character, and His lifestyle. When families are only partially surrendered to God they are open to all types of lifestyles and strongholds. We may take our relationships with God for granted as evidenced by us rationalizing our family members' behaviors or lifestyles.

We cannot hug and kiss the opposite sex and think that it's ok, especially when the Bible teaches us, *Now concerning the things whereof ye wrote unto me: It is good for a man not to touch a woman* 1 Corinthians 7:1, (KJV);You ask, "Why? Or, say it's not that serious." Solomon warns us, *Can a man take fire in his bosom, and his clothes not be burned? Can one go upon hot coals, and his feet not be burned?* Proverbs 6:27-28, (KJV).

We cannot entertain the world and not be consumed by it. When we entertain worldly living, no matter how right we think it may seem, or how we feel about it, it is unhealthy for the family and their relationships with one another. Amos 3:3 (KJV), *Can two walk together, except they be agreed?*

The family cannot walk or live the blueprint of God if they do not walk by the rules of God. Families cannot walk by God's rules if we do not actually know the rules. So many families today, struggle, because we are not steadfast. To be truly steadfast and strong family members as well as the family must study the word of God. 2 Timothy 2:15, (KJV), says, *Study to show thyself approved unto God a workman that needeth not to be ashamed, rightly dividing the word of truth.*

Healthy Families

I love talking about the healthy family because it gives us the very hope and vision that we all desire for our families. Sometimes to develop and maintain healthy families it requires us to exercise tough love. Tough love is one tool that we, parents, will usually only implement as a last resort. However, the Lord shows tough love to His children as stated in Hebrews 12:6, (NLT); *For the Lord disciplines those He loves, and he punishes those he accepts as his children.*

Tough love for me is just another term for Grace. Grace is God's unmerited favor. It is receiving love when we don't deserve it. Our families don't deserve God's love and yet He charges us to love one another as He has loved us, John 13:34 (NLT), *So now I am giving you a new commandment: Love each other. Just as I have loved you, you should love each other.*

Yes, that's good healthy stuff. God loves us in spite of all of our mess. Then He calls for us to love the rest of the family members with the same love that he has displayed to you and me. Love is essential; this is the attribute that we are challenged to walk in. It's why we can stand firm with our family members when it seems as if they are becoming unstable in their walk with God and his word. God's love is why and how we can be steadfast with our family members when everything seems to be falling down around us.

It's not that I don't love my children when I call them on their sexual behaviors, their entertaining the lifestyles of this world or any other ungodly behavior. In fact, if I love them as Christ loves me, I must call their behavior to their attention. If they fail to listen to me as their parent, I must exercise the truths in the following scriptures to keep the family healthy.

1. Galatians 6:1 (KJV), *Brethren, if a man be overtaken in a fault, ye which are spiritual, restore such a one in the spirit of meekness; considering thyself, lest thou also be tempted.*

   We must show compassion to our loved one to open the door of restoration. Healthy families do not use harshness in restoring a loved one, rather they show compassion (sympathy) to the one that needs it.

2. Matthew 18:21-22 (NLT), *Then Peter came to him and asked, "Lord, how often should I forgive someone who sins against me? Seven times?" "No!" Jesus replied, "seventy times seven!"*

   What happens when you show compassion and the loved one continues to display the same behavior or lifestyle? Our compassion, through forgiveness, must continually be displayed to the one who is in need of it. Jesus' reply means 7x70 which is 490 times in a day. This is an excellent example of how we should extend grace to everyone.

   Even though someone is forgiven the appropriate discipline is always in order. In fact, we can learn a lesson from the father and his son who decided to disrespect his father with his attitude.

   And he said, a certain man has two sons: And the younger of them said to his father, Father, give me the portion of goods that falleth to me, And he divided unto them his living Luke 15:11-12, (KJV). How can we expect something or demand anything when we have not worked for it?

And not many days after the younger son gathered all together, and took his journey into a far country; and there wasted his substance with riotous living. Luke 15:13, (KJV). He spent all of his father's earnings, which is another form of disrespect.

And when he had spent all, there arose a mighty famine in that land; and he began to be in want. And he went and joined himself to a citizen of that country; and he sent him into the fields to feed swine. Luke 15:14-15, (KJV). He began to live like the world which was another form of disrespect to his father, especially after his father had spent years teaching him the right way to live. How children conduct themselves away from home is a strong reflection on their parents and home life.

And he would fain have filled his belly with the husks that the swine did eat; and no man gave unto him. And when he came to himself, he said, How many hired servants of my father's have bread enough and to spare, and I perish with hunger! Luke 15:16-17, (KJV). Our children will frequently come to themselves after they have gone through some tough situations, but that is not the problem here. The problem is, what will you do when they return?

I will arise and go to my father, and will say unto him, Father, I have sinned against heaven, and before thee, And am no more worthy to be called thy son: make me as one of thy hired servant. Luke 15:18-19, (KJV). When our children realize what they have done to the family and to God, in most cases, they will return with a repentant heart. It's like the child who stole from you for his next fix, or the child who left the family for some crazy romance that caused them to become promiscuous, or the child who got caught up running with the wrong company. When they come to themselves and return with a repentant heart, will you receive them with God's love? Will you be ready to minister to them?

Let's see what his father did upon the son's return. *And he arose, and came to his father. But when he was yet a great way off, his father saw him, and had compassion, and ran, and fell on his neck, and kissed him. Luke 15:20, (KJV).* The father was looking for his son to return and when he saw his son he ran to meet him. The father, welcomed his son back with total forgiveness and unconditional love. In fact it was as if his son had not done anything wrong.

And the son said unto him, Father, I have sinned against heaven, and in thy sight, and am no more worthy to be called thy son. But the father said to his servant, Bring forth the best robe, and put it on him, and put a ring on his hand, and shoes on his feet: And bring hither the fatted calf, and kill it; and let us eat, and be merry: For this my son was dead, and is alive again; he was lost, and is found. And they began to be merry. Luke 15:21-24, (KJV). The father celebrated over his son's heart of repentance.

Our children often times never feel this type of celebration because we have allowed their sin to become our sin. If we cannot release their past behavior and lifestyle, then how do we expect God to restore the family to health?

3. 1 Corinthians 3:17 (KJV), *If any man defile the temple of God, him shall God destroy; for the temple of God is holy, which temple ye are.*

One more lesson can be learned from this father, and it may be painful for some and for some just down right unheard of. The time may come when we have to release our children from our homes if they choose not to follow the rules that have been placed as guidelines for the health of the family.

Now I know this may sound totally ridiculous. You can't put your child out when they are minors. Says who? If a child at the age of fifteen cannot follow the rules, yes, it is time to allow him to have what he or she is asking for. Even God allows us the right to choose. We may have to suffer the consequences but he allows us to live any way we see fit, and he will have nothing to do with sin.

A separation as far as living quarters may be necessary. Even when a physical separation occurs, a separation from the heart should never occur. *Wherefore come out from among them, and be ye separate, saith the Lord, and touch not the unclean thing; and I will receive you.* 2 Corinthians 6:17 (KJV).

If we don't release them then the family may become unhealthy. Most likely other siblings in the home will strive to be just like the one who refuses to keep in step with the rules of the house.

But if we allow the one who has chosen to live in sin to pack up his or her sins and move out, the house will stabilize and return to a healthy state. Prayerfully, the one who has left will soon come to his or her senses and return home with a repentant heart.

This is tough love at its best. God loves us enough to let us go, only to love us back unto

> himself. While our child is out of the home we are to continue to love him or her.
>
> Here are some ways to love them back into God's arms, and back into the family. Prayer is a vital element of love. Sometimes fasting is required. Parents, we must prepare our hearts for the return of our children so that we will not be like the brother who stayed home and dealt with his brother based on his sins. The brother who stayed home should have followed his father's lead and received his brother back with forgiveness and unconditional love.

I have been down this road with my two sons. I will never forget how my wife and I felt when our two sons were given the option to pull themselves together and follow the rules of the house or to move out. They were 15 years old at the time, and just like many other young people that age, they thought they knew what was best for them.

They left the home to live with their biological father in another state. My wife's heart and my heart were in pain. Even our daughter missed her brothers tremendously. We had no idea where we went wrong. We began to pray about what we were to do about this, if anything at all. The Lord said, "Prepare yourselves, for their return. The worst thing about this would be when I bring them home and you are not prepared for them spiritually." So we began to spend more and more time praying and seeking God's face for instructions on what we needed to do.

Our sons came home to visit after a year. When they left going back to their father the hurt and pain revisited us.

Little did we know that this was God's way of equipping us for their return. We had never had a heartfelt family time until then. This does not mean that we were not spending time together in prayer as a family. It was that we had not truly opened up our hearts to each other to understand where each member was spiritually.

You will be amazed at what you don't know about where your family is with God and His word. We went to church. In fact, I was the pastor of the church and believed that I knew. How could I not know exactly where my family was with God? I never thought that there was a problem. We were a family that prayed together. We had done street ministry together, our children sang in the choir, and my wife worked in the church. So, how could we not know how each other was with God? We thought we were the ideal family until this separation came about.

When our sons returned home after a year to visit for about two weeks in the summer they had lost weight and looked malnourished. They were spiritually malnourished too. Our sons had gone to church only once during the year they were away from home. Before they left home they went to church at least three days a week. On Sunday they attended Sunday School, morning worship and sometime an evening service. On Monday they attended choir rehearsal and Wednesday they attended Prayer Meetings and Bible Study.

God had truly prepared us for their return. We had gone to a Christian book store and purchased age appropriate Bible Study literature. The house was full of their favorite foods. The boys were involved in a Bible Study nine evenings out the two weeks and the other five evenings we were at church. I know this might sound like over kill. But remember they were spiritually malnourished and we only had two weeks to nourish them back to health. We fed our sons physical food until they were full and satisfied. Our goal was to also get them full and satisfied on spiritual food. They responded to the Bible Studies like hungry babies sucking milk from bottles. Their response was a perfect example of 1 Peter 2:2, (KJV); *As new born babes, desire the sincere milk of the word, that ye may grow thereby.*

By the time the visit was almost over the boys asked could they come back for Christmas. Of course our answer was yes. They returned to their father's home. Within a week our sons called and asked could they come back home to stay. Of course our answer was yes, with the understanding that the rules were the same as when they left. They clearly understood. Our children returned home to stay, our family time changed. We began to spend time talking about the life and times of each member. We started reassuring one another that we were there for each other, and that God was there for all of us.

Now one would think that we would never have to revisit this area of our lives again. Wrong. We did revisit the area with one of our sons when he was age 22. He was wrestling with growing from a young man into an adult. I had to ask my son to leave our home again because of his behavior in the home. He left and about a year later he returned, with a repentant heart and a renewed attitude.

He said something to me and his mother that helped us see God with different eyes. "I know from having you as my parents that God's love is real. For the way that I have treated the both of you and my brother and my sister

I should never be allowed back in the house. But you both loved me in spite of what I had done. That helped me realize that God is real and he is worthy of my life."

My family members are now more solid in their walks with God than ever before. Man, what a blessing it is to hear your children truly open up and talk about their most private battles. We talk about these types of issues so that we can pray for each other, be a leaning post for each other, and most of all speak into each others' lives with the word of God. This has helped us to develop into a healthy family. Maintaining a healthy family requires constant work with open communication between all family members.

Here are four points to consider. These will help you keep your family healthy.

1. Give Godly guidance.

    Titus gives us great instruction on how we are to give godly guidance to the family. Titus 2:1-8 (NLT) *But as for you, promote the kind of living that reflects right teaching. Teach the older men to exercise self-control, to be worthy of respect, and to live wisely. They must have strong faith and be filled with love and patience.*

    Similarly, teach the older women to live in a way that is appropriate for someone serving the Lord. They must not go around speaking evil of others and must not be heavy drinkers. Instead, they should teach others what is good. These older women must train the younger women to love their husbands and their children, to live wisely and be pure, to take care of their home, to do good, and to be submissive to their husbands. Then they will not bring shame on the word of God.

In the same way, encourage the young men to live wisely in all they do. And you yourself must be an example to them by doing good deeds of every kind. Let everything you do reflect the integrity and seriousness of your teaching. Let your teaching be so correct that it can't be criticized. Then those who want to argue will be ashamed because they won't have anything bad to say about us.

Paul is instructing us to take the time to deposit what is in us as parents into our children. Teach them, be a model for them, and display our integrity with high standards.

2. Increase your intimacy.

Jesus helps us here in Matthew 22:37-39, (NLT); *Jesus replied, "'You must love the Lord your God with all your heart, all your soul, and all your mind.' This is first and greatest commandment. A second is equally important: 'Love your neighbor as yourself….'*

Jesus gives us the rule for living as a healthy family. He teaches us that we first must love God with everything we have within us, and second, to love others like we love ourselves.

A normal man does not hate himself, instead loves himself enough that he will do all he can to make things right for himself. That is the attribute that is needed in keeping the family healthy.

You may ask why I am using God so much in this book? I do that because God is the author of intimacy. He is forever into us, whether we are into him or not. According to the above text he has placed the ability to love and the ability to receive love into our families. That is the basis of the blueprint. It is having someone or something to follow to arrive at a state of health.

3. Educate your children.

When we have been afforded the opportunity to increase our knowledge and to equip ourselves for a better physical and social life, we should take full advantage of this opportunity. We also must know that education in the physical sense is not enough, nor all that is required for us to have healthy families.

We need to be educated on who God is and what he has deposited into us to make it possible for us to learn and use our minds. Romans 12:1-2 (NLT), *And so, dear brothers and sisters, I plead with you to give your bodies to God. Let them be a living and holy sacrifice-the kind he will accept. When you think of what he has done for you, is this too much to ask? Don't copy the behavior and customs of this world, but let God transform* (change your condition, your nature, and your function) *you into a new person by changing the way you think. Then you will know what God wants you to do, and you will know how good and pleasing and perfect his will really is.*

Here God helps us to keep things in balance in our family life as well as our personal lives. Without learning about God we shall become like this world which is materialistic. Often materialism divides the family because of work, sports, social clubs and other associations.

We must get involved with our children's education for it helps build the soundness of the family and the lives of our children. When we invest in their education, both secular and spiritual, our children will almost always look for ways to give back to the family that it may remain healthy.

4. Understand the purpose of dating.

   We train our children according to the blueprint by being models they can see of a man and woman interacting with each other. Our children watch our lives, as parents, and how we model relationships with each other. Our children closely watch how we honor each other, how we respect each other, how we speak into each others' lives and how we lift each other up. The purpose of dating is to learn what health is by observing solid relationships and modeling what is observed.

   Through this model children learn what a healthy relationship looks like and what it takes to keep it healthy. They also learn that the relationship which the family was birthed from was never based on sex, rather, on honoring and loving one's self, one's family, and God.

Use these four principles as your foundation for building a healthy family. Please understand these four principles alone will not work without God's help. They come from his blueprint for the family and no one can make these principles operate better than Him.

Father God, help us today as we build on each others lives, that we may experience your divine power and structure for our family.

My heart's desire is that families will embrace old school teachings about the family, its principles and legacies. Oh, I know that is a bit old fashioned, but I am convinced there are some things from the past that should never be forgotten.

I am a TV buff who loves, to watch family shows. These shows teach us the importance of family and what will happen if we don't invest in the lives of our family members.

I hope and pray this book will help some families experience God's true and wonderful design for the family.

I hope and pray this book will provide tools that will encourage families to build and grow according to God's blueprint and produce strong healthy families.